such purposes, they can withstand the same amount of terrible weather when converted into a home. These shipping containers can be placed in almost any climate if they are equipped with the right insulations and temperature control features.

Lead Time

The expected time frame for a single-family home is around seven months. This is exceptionally long when compared to the average of three months it takes to complete a container home. Shipping container homes are created and built much faster because the majority of the heavy lifting is already done. When you buy a shipping container with the purpose of converting it, it is already equipped with a roof, floor, and walls. These reasons make the lead time much faster for both bigger and smaller shipping container projects.

Customizable

A shipping container home can easily be customized, with a variety of ways to build and create; the possibilities are endless. Because we are all different, your shipping container home can reflect this as well, whether you decide to create different sizes on the top and bottom floor or want the house to be wider than it is long. The beauty of building with shipping containers is that there are virtually no limits to the designs you can create.

With an eye on your personal style and taste, you can create the perfect home with or without the help of a professional. When building with shipping containers, you are not limited to the same rules as traditional building methods—think of them as building blocks! This way of building gives complete creative freedom, and you can craft even the most intricate of designs, as your shipping container home can be custom-built to any specification. A prime example of this can be seen on websites like loveproperty.com, which showcases some of the most unique and stunning designs that have been created by architects and homeowners. Although most people choose a homesite and build with the intention of staying there for a long time, shipping container homes can also be moved to different locations. The moveability of your project will, however, depend on the design and the way that the shipping containers are fastened to the foundation.

Carbon Footprint

Although not all shipping container homes are eco-friendly, it is entirely possible to create a container home that has a very low carbon footprint. This can easily be achieved by making small decisions that impact the world in a big way. These choices range from solar panels to rainwater collection tanks. Since shipping container homes are used for off-the-grid living a majority of the time, there are significant ways to minimize the upkeep costs for this way of living.

Chapter 2: The Key Aspects of a Container Home

Insulation

Insulation is one of the most important aspects of a successful build. Since shipping containers are made from solid steel, it is prone to extreme cold and heat on the inside, and this can drive your electric bill up significantly. A very well-kept secret of the shipping container industry is that you can buy shipping containers that are already insulated. Some items that cross the ocean need to be kept at certain temperatures. Because of this simple fact, there are a multitude of shipping containers for sale that have most of the conversion legwork already done.

If you can't find an already insulated shipping container, you will need to install this yourself. Each of the options for insulation comes with their own benefits and cost to the consumer.

Types of Insulation:

Insulation is governed by an R-factor rating, this rating will determine how effective the insulation material is at insulating. The highest R-factor you can buy is R-45 and the lowest is R-0.

Always check the R-factor on an insulation product before buying it.

Spray Foam

Foam insulation works by spraying a coating of the semi-permeable foam directly against the steel walls of the shipping container. As one of the most used and widely recommended forms of insulation, spray foam is by far one of the best options for insulating a shipping container. Regardless of the possible cost setbacks, this remains the absolute best option for quality insulation.

The Positives:

This foam is very pliable and will adapt to any size or shape, and may offer a better chance to get creative with the internal or external shape of your walls. It also forms a tight seal that keeps any moisture or air from penetrating it. The majority of prefabricated shipping container homes will be equipped and installed using this method of insulation.

The Negatives:

This type of insulation can be time-consuming and expensive since it is not DIY-friendly. Installation has to be done by professionals as the gas can be somewhat poisonous and toxic. It is incredibly important to have proper ventilation and safety wear when near the site as it is being installed.

Glass Wool Insulation Blanket

This type of insulation is the most affordable and easiest to find. The glass wool insulation blanket is available in both pre-cut batts and rolls. It is a mineral or fiberglass insulator that is made from recycled rock and glass. The rock and glass are melted down and spun into the final product.

The Positives:

This type of insulation is completely renewable and eco-friendly. There are many thermal benefits, and because the product traps air, it is virtually fireproof. This type of insulation has been tested by more than a 1000 independent studies, and it is also completely approved by the World Health Organization. It is also the absolute cheapest type of insulation.

The Negatives:

It is of the utmost importance to wear gloves and masks when coming into contact with this product, as it is made from spun stone and glass. This product can easily damage skin or cause trouble breathing if inhaled. Because of its natural shape, there are always gaps between where the batts or rolls are laid, and these tiny gaps can cause heat loss. Over time, the product will also start to sag and compress, and this causes further gaps and significant heat loss. This product can also harbor wetness and condensation which may be exacerbated by the metal of the containers themselves. The only way to fix water or moisture damage to this type of insulation is to replace it completely, and this can cause it to become very expensive. If you have the budget for a better insulation, it may be more cost-effective in the long run to buy something else.

Insulation Panels

This type of insulation consists of two composite panels that sandwich an insulation barrier, such as an air or vapor barrier.

The Positives:

This type of insulation can be made directly to the dimensions of your walls and this makes sure you won't have any wasted material. Combining this type of insulation with an air barrier or vapor barrier can also yield incredible results, as this will play a key role in the longevity of your shipping container home by ensuring that no rust or corrosion occurs. Insulation panels are very energy efficient because of their capability to control the temperature, and are also more versatile and cost-effective, because the right product does not need to be covered with wood or drywall.

The Negatives:

There are many great benefits, however the negatives might overshadow them. These panels are prone to moisture, and in an enclosed space like a shipping container this can be detrimental. These panels are also not airtight if used on their own without a suitable air barrier, because they don't fit the natural shape of the shipping container walls. This method of insulation can become quite costly purely because both the insulation panels and an air barrier will need to be fitted.

Eco-Friendly Insulation Materials

This type of insulation is the absolute best for keeping a container home completely eco-friendly. There are several types of insulation that are considered eco-friendly, and some of the most common are made from straw bales, sheep's wool, or natural cotton. Another option is most commonly seen in a product like aerogel. Aerogel is a solid material that has an extremely low density which is produced by removing the liquid components from traditional gel. The main examples of these insulators are Cellulose, EPS foam board, Closed-cell spray foam insulation, Magnesium oxide, and Vacuum Insulated Panels (VIP).

The Positives:

This type of insulation is completely safe for humans and is non-toxic, so there is no risk of adverse health effects. These work best when used mainly for thermal control.

The Negatives:

These types of insulation materials are easy to install, but they are incredibly flammable. In a shipping container home, one of the main things you want to avoid is flammable materials as the metal walls will conduct heat very well.

Recycled Materials

This form of insulation is often referred to as cellulose insulation and is generally made out of recycled newspaper;

other forms include plastic and denim. This solution is best for temperature control and not complete insulation.

The Positives:

These types of insulators are easy to find and generally cost-efficient. You can install these easily and there is no need for extreme safety equipment.

The Negatives:

Unfortunately, this type of insulation is prone to pests, mold, and dampness. It is also very flammable and can become dangerous quite easily.

Plastered Finish

This is a form of insulation usually made from clay, cement, or sand and sand plaster. This is a very affordable way to insulate a home and also allows for some creativity in shaping the inside or outside of your home. For the best insulation results, avoid using a plastered finish in cold and wet areas, and research on the best combination for your area. Using cement plaster on the inside and clay on the outside can yield great results. This type of finish is not recommended for cold and wet areas not only because plaster needs a while to set, but also because the components in plaster can freeze fairly easily. Cold and wet areas will reduce the effectiveness of the product and can cause it to not set completely or at all.

Vapor Barriers

Vapor barriers are materials used to stop water droplets like condensation that can be detrimental to the health of the steel, because they cause fast deterioration of the steel and can lead to rust.

These barriers will not only protect the steel, but also the interior furnishing such as wood or drywall. The best option for this is wraps, like Tyvek wraps. This wrap looks and feels like paper but is actually made from high-density polyethylene fibers. This wrap is incredibly strong and is hard to tear but can easily be cut with sharp scissors or carpentry knives.

This barrier will significantly decrease the amount of vapor, but the only way to completely eradicate it is by using a foam insulator.

Heating and Cooling

Although insulators can play a significant role in keeping the greenhouse effect of a shipping container home at bay, it is important to employ the added benefit of a heating and cooling system. This section will only be of use for normal shipping container conversion; in the case where an already insulated or refrigerated shipping container is bought, these systems will already be installed.

There are many ways to control the temperature in shipping containers, but as most people building container homes are focused on cost-effective methods of building, we're going to discuss using non-traditional forms of heating and cooling. One way is using radiant barriers that direct the sunlight away from the roof of your shipping container home. It is best to use reflective paints or materials for this purpose, but you may also utilize solar panels to get the most out of the available energy.

Another very effective way to go about maintaining the temperature of your home is to make use of a living roof or rooftop garden. A living roof or green roof is a type of temperature control system, normally seen as a house that is partially or completely covered in vegetation, which is becoming a massive trend in the shipping container home industry.

These are incredible at keeping heat at bay, and this way of temperature control is environmentally friendly and makes the space look beautiful. A nice garden feeling can be created by placing grass and small blooming flowers like roses and forget-me-nots. Other ideas can also be implemented by placing flowering vines and such along the perimeter of the shipping container roof. Because of the impressive strength of a shipping container shell, a green roof can also be used as a place to escape to. This can easily be achieved by placing chairs or outdoor lounge sets on a grass base. Privacy can be created on this roof by placing rose bushes and other big plant species along the perimeter that faces the road or neighbors.

The Exterior

Shipping containers come in a variety of sizes. The most common ones are 8 ft wide and 8.5 ft high; lengthwise you can find them in either 20 ft or 40 ft. Shipping containers also come in high-cube options that are 9.5 ft high; these containers are more expensive but give more room for insulation. Shipping containers can also be bought in sizes between 8 ft and 10 ft; these sizes are rare but work incredibly well when used as bathroom add-ons to your main container home.

It is a good idea to have a container home run on solar panels and to have a system that can harvest rainwater. Although neither of these are necessary, both options can make living in a container home cheaper.

The exterior decorating of a container home is entirely up to personal preference and can be done in a multitude of ways. By incorporating a lush garden or a swimming pool made out of another container, you can easily make the space beautiful.

The Interior

In recent years, tiny living has become a craze that took the world by storm. Container homes can fall into this category, and many of the tips and tricks used by tiny living professionals can be applied to most container homes with great results. Predominately, this involves clever storage spaces, loft beds, and fold out tables.

Of course, if you are building a larger container home, these space-saving designs might not be necessary. You could decorate the interior as you would any traditional home, or even choose to leave a section of the container uncovered as a type of feature wall.

Chapter 3: The Building Process

Deciding on living in a container home is a big decision and there are a lot of elements that go into such a house. There is a vast amount of information out there regarding the how and what of container homes, but the ultimate question is "Where do I start?"

Step One: Paperwork and Legality

Before any planning around a shipping container home can start, the question of legality is important.

Shipping containers have been used in construction and as temporary offices for a long time, but there are still no steadfast rules regarding these buildings that apply nationwide. That means that a bit of research on the rules and regulations in your area will need to happen before you get started. Luckily, in most states and counties, it is completely legal to build a container home, if the land is owned.

Before investing in any property or shipping container, it is important to note the following rules that need to be obeyed:

Property Zoning Laws

Zoning committees, at their core, are regulatory bodies that control which areas can have certain types of buildings. When deciding on a shipping container home, it is important to find out from the zoning committee if the property is suitable for such a building. The zoning committee is the first obstacle before any other planning can commence.

Finding out if your property is suited for a shipping container home is as easy as visiting the office of your local zoning commission or looking up your city or county's website online.

The rules and regulations of each committee differ; while Houston in Texas has very few laws around this, Tallahassee in Florida has a multitude of different laws.

Building Permits and Codes

Building codes and permits are wildly diverse in every state, therefore it is of the utmost importance to research the laws that apply to your specific town.

Many states have policies that are built on the International Residential Code (IRC) and the International Building Code (IBC). These codes and permits encompass everything, from the plumbing and electrical codes to mechanical codes and fire protection acts.

Websites like constructconnect.com offer a search function that immediately gives details of the codes and permits you need to apply for, but contacting an architect or general contractor can give you a clearer picture.

It is of utmost importance to sort all permits and regulations out before investing any money into buying supplies, land, or shipping containers.

Mobile, Manufactured, and Modular Building Codes

Discerning which type of building code authority you need to follow can be hard; most homes that are not created on site will fall into the following categories:

- **Mobile and Manufactured Homes**

A manufactured home is a new name for what was originally called a mobile home. The name was changed in 1976, but both names refer to homes mounted on a permanent trailer chassis.

These homes are covered under the HUD regulations or U.S. Department of Housing and Urban Development regulations. This code is the only code that is regulated by the federal government and it only applies to houses that are entirely built in a factory and then moved to the permanent site.

- **Modular Homes**

Modular homes—in which building modules are built in a factory, then transported to the site and assembled on a permanent foundation—usually fall under the International Building Code (IBC), not the HUD code.

The route you take when it comes to the construction of the home determines the authority you will need to contact. Both options are completely viable, but the costs involved can vary dramatically.

Deed Restrictions and HomeOwners Associations (HOA)

The majority of zoning laws and regulations are government-issued or enforced, but there is one last regulatory body that needs to be discussed. Both deed restrictions and HOA's are put into place to protect property value and to create a uniform appearance in neighborhoods.

These entities can refuse a shipping container home in the neighborhood they oversee, and the only way to bypass them is by either a controlled vote by the HOA or a court order to remove a deed restriction.

Because of all these factors, it is recommended to see a lawyer that is familiar with zoning and property rules. Going this route takes a lot of stress out of the planning portion and can simplify getting all of the permits and avoiding any legal repercussions.

All of these restrictions, rules, and regulations apply to all types of building and the expenses of these permits, codes, and inspections are universal across traditional buildings as well as shipping container homes.

Step Two: DIY, Prefab, or Hiring a Contractor?

There are a multitude of ways to go about getting your dream shipping container home built. The route of building depends on personal preference, your budget, and the amount of knowledge one possesses on a certain area of construction.

Do it Yourself

When it comes to container building, going the DIY route can be incredibly hard. There are a lot of aspects to consider including the plumbing, insulation, the electrical system, and the possible connection of containers to each other.

Some aspects are a lot easier to DIY, and these include some of the decor and general aesthetic of the shipping container home.

Another key aspect that can be done yourself is the insulation of the walls and flooring. With proper research, many components of a container home can be done yourself, however if you don't have the proper tools or are not familiar with the processes, it can quickly become an expensive and tedious project.

Prefabricated

A prefabricated container home is created in a warehouse by a company that specializes in such buildings. This route can be expensive but offers the guarantee that everything in the shipping container is done correctly. The possible downside to this form of building is that you may not have any say in the types of materials used to create your home.

For this route to work best, it is important to do research on the company and inquire into the kinds of materials they use, what customizations are possible, and what design options are offered. This method of building a shipping container home is generally a bit more expensive than it would be to build the entire structure yourself, but knowing that everything inside is done up to code means that you can be sure your house is safe and will pass inspection.

Hiring a Contractor

This method of building is what you might refer to as a happy medium. With the cost benefit of doing it yourself, and the knowledge of an expert, this method can help give you an exceptional structure without being charged exorbitant prices. A contractor is usually also knowledgeable in local building codes and regulations and may also be able to acquire materials at a lower cost than if you buy them yourself.

For this route to be most beneficial, it is wise to hire a general contractor that already knows how to work with shipping containers, as incorrect methods can damage the exterior of the container.

Step Three: Preparations

At this stage of the process, it is time to ensure that all of the necessary preparations are in order. It is important to ensure that adequate preparations are made before the container/s are delivered.

The Budget

It is of utmost importance to set a budget. Your budget should cover every aspect of building your shipping container home and detail every dollar that you will spend. Key elements that should be included in the budgets are:

● Design elements: Internal fixtures and furnishings (plumbing, lighting, kitchen, and bathroom) and external design elements.

● Furniture: When creating a budget, add a section for the furniture you will buy. As shipping container homes have smaller internal areas to work with, you may end up having to specially buy furniture that fits in your new home.

● Contractor fees: This includes every person that will work on your project, including engineers, architects, welders, and so on.

● Buying: Include all costs that correlate with buying of containers, land, materials, etc.

It's also a good idea to include a contingency budget. This is a sum of money that is put away for any emergencies or unforeseen building expenses. As a general rule of thumb for all building projects, the recommendation is to put away at least 20% of the expected total cost of the project. If the project is very creative or complex, more than 20% is recommended. As an example, if you can only spend $200,000 on the entire project, $160,000 would go in the primary budget and 20% (or $40,000) would be put in the contingency budget.

Crafting a budget can be exceptionally hard, and because of this, we have included a sample budget later this book. In that section, all of the tips, tricks, and explanations will guide you through the process of compiling your budget.

The Plan

Once you have the budget down, the next step is to create a floor plan. This can be accomplished by drawing it by hand on a piece of paper or using design software like planner 5D. The first plan you draw should only serve as a guideline to how you see your future shipping container home put together. The complete house plan is better off being drafted by an industry professional as there are many detailed aspects to creating a house plan.

Step Four: Purchasing

After successfully securing the required documentation, we can begin looking at properties and shipping containers.

Shipping Containers

Buying a shipping container is a lot like buying a car, we need to inspect each aspect of the shipping container to ensure that the best financial choices are made.

1. Size: There are many sizes to choose from, the main ones being either a 20 ft or 40 ft container. Once the size is agreed upon, as well as how many containers you may want to purchase for your design, it is time to move on to a more physical approach.

2. Research: The sad fact of today's society is that nothing can be taken at face value; always research the company you will buy from. Research will determine if the seller is reputable and if they will deliver the product as agreed. You may have a great piece of land picked out, but if the container won't be delivered there by the company, you may have to look into other transportation for your future home. Always pay close attention to reviews about sellers and companies, as this can tell you a great deal about them.

3. Inspection: Inspecting a container is incredibly important, whether it is a one-time sea traveler or if it has been around the sea-ports a few times. Start by closing the door and inspecting the inside in the dark; if any light peeks through, the container has holes and is not suitable for conversion. If the container has

many deep dents or rust, it is also advised to not buy it. A shipping container is a lot cheaper than traditional buildings, but you will still spend quite an amount of money converting it, therefore it is of the utmost importance to buy a container that is in great shape. Next check the CSC, this is a type of inspection that is primarily used for shipping containers. The CSC is stamped on a metal plate that is attached to the door of the shipping container. These plates are generally removed when the containers are used for storage or conversions, the CSC is used as a type of certification. This certification is generally used to give the green light and to show that the ISO/Shipping container is up to standard.

4. Delivery: Pay attention to what your delivery costs cover. Moving a shipping container isn't cheap, and companies can easily trick you into paying for a service that doesn't include everything you need.

5. Paint: Finding a container that is freshly painted might sound like a bargain, but in reality, containers are often painted before a sale in order to hide rust. Small patches of rust aren't that big of a deal and can be easily remedied, but if a container is thoroughly rusted, it could cost more to fix the rust than the container is worth.

There are a few rules when buying a container, and the most obvious is the grading of the container. Containers are graded in four categories: A, B, C and Food-grade. Categories A and food-grade are the best to buy for conversion, purely because of future cost-effectiveness.

The younger a container is, the better. Usually category A and food-grade containers have had the least trips on the sea and have suffered the least damage, but it is none-the-less important to inspect them thoroughly. These types of containers are the cheapest to convert but usually cost more in the initial purchase.

Property

After checking to make sure that the shipping container is the absolute best value for your money, it is important to check if your property is eligible.

In order to be certain that your property is suitable, there are a few things that you need to pay close attention to.

An incredibly important first step is to survey the composition of the land. There are many components to soil, and some of these components are detrimental to building, such as various types of sand.

- Silt: This component of sand is incredibly fine; it can be sand, clay, or any other organic material. Silt is easily carried by water, and if it exceeds the threshold of making up 8% of the ground, it can cause structural problems if it is washed away by rain or surface water.

● Clay: This natural soil composition is detrimental to building, especially in wet and rainy environments. When water mixes with the clay deposits in the soil, it can create a change on a molecular level, which can cause the foundation to sink away or air pockets to form underneath the foundation.

● Beach or River sand: This can cause many problems if this sand comes into contact with water. These types of sand are not suitable for building a foundation on as they are not at all stable and will cause the foundation to collapse.

Not many people are aware of the issues that can arise due to the soil that they build on. Luckily, if analysis shows any of the above-mentioned soil types, there is a very easy fix.

According to the experts at Azagneiss, a quarry that specializes in sand, the fix is as easy as removing the problematic ground on the part where the foundation should be. Once that area is excavated, the whole foundation can be filled with G5 and G6 filling material.

These materials are the best for building a foundation on, as they are specifically created with just enough fine and rough material to give you the absolute best results when you are building. However, the easiest option is obviously to purchase a piece of land that is suitable from building on right from the start!

Step Five: Modifications

One of the biggest attractions to building a shipping container home is the unlimited creative freedom it offers. These homes can be turned into whatever the owner imagines.

In theory, it is extremely easy to cut holes into the steel box that is a shipping container, but in reality, it is much more complex than that. Shipping containers are built in such a way that they are strengthened at the corners. Because of this, reinforcements will be needed for each and every hole that is cut into the steel.

There are a multitude of ways to modify and reinforce the steel walls of a shipping container. One of the most common ways is by cutting large holes in the side panels to create big windows, as this will make the interior of the shipping container feel connected to the outside and appear much bigger. Generally speaking, the part where the doors open on a container that has not been altered will be the space most contractors put their doors, as putting doors anywhere other than the end or side would be highly impractical. For instance, given that a shipping container is not very wide, it would take up a lot of space to implement something like a rooftop door.

Another very popular option when building with shipping containers is to remove an entire side panel and to install a very large sliding door. Building this way gives you a lot more freedom over space. If the big sliding door opens up onto a patio, you can extend the living area into the outdoors.

Step Six: On-Site Preparations

Once the decisions have been made, it is time to prepare the site for the shipping container delivery.

How To: The Foundation

The foundation is arguably the most important aspect of the entire building process, because ground can move and shift. When ground moves and shifts it can have an immense impact on how level your home is.

There are four main types of foundations that are used when building shipping container homes:

Pier Foundation:

This type of foundation is the most popular, because of its inexpensive and DIY-friendly nature. A pier foundation consists of concrete blocks; these blocks are usually 50 cm x 50 cm x 50 cm. These piers are usually placed at each of the four corners; two additional piers can be installed for longer containers.

It is easy to install these piers because very little ground needs to be excavated. By only digging the holes for the piers and using steel to reinforce the piers, this type of foundation is incredibly stable and strong.

Pile Foundation:

This type of foundation is mostly used in cases where the soil is too weak to bear the weight of a complete concrete base, and this is also the most expensive foundation type.

Piles are solid, cylindrical steel tubes. These tubes are hammered into the ground, past the soft soil, until harder soil is reached. This type of foundation is not at all DIY-friendly and a contractor is needed to install this type.

Slab Foundation:

This type of foundation is mainly used on soft soil. This uses the technique of distributing the weight of the shipping container evenly over the soil. This type of foundation is a lot more time consuming because of the time needed to allow the concrete to cure and is also much more expensive.

A big downside of this type of foundation is that an entire concrete slab needs to be laid down. Before it is possible to pour concrete, a foundation has to be dug out. This time-consuming activity can cost a lot in terms of contractors and equipment.

The concrete slab has to be bigger than the outline of the shipping container and generally should include a patio area. This task is very difficult to complete when going DIY and therefore piles are recommended. There is, however, one aspect that can't be overlooked, which is that a slab provides a completely filled foundation. When foundations have gaps underneath the house, such as in a pile or pier foundation, it can create a breeding ground for termites and other pests.

Strip Foundation:

This foundation type is a mix of a slab and pier foundation. This foundation type combines the positives of both and reduces the negative impacts that often happen with going just one route. Strips are essentially a strip of concrete that is placed where the shipping container will go. The strips can go around the perimeter of the container or can be used only on the top and bottom of the container perimeters.

This form works best when the ground is soft and there is a need for a slab foundation, since they essentially serve the same purpose.

How To: Attaching Shipping Containers to the Foundation

The easiest way, and the process most revered by the building community, to attach a shipping container to the foundation is by using a steel plate. This route offers a cast-in steel plate that is pressed underneath wet concrete so the anchors to hold the container in place are the only part visible above the concrete. It is also becoming increasingly popular to use epoxy to set the anchors in dried concrete. The final option is to use mechanical anchors. These anchors are typically less strong, and therefore aren't recommended.

Most people then place the container on the steel plate in the concrete, and weld the anchors to the shipping container. It is also possible to just place the container on a foundation, having nothing but the heavy weight to hold the container in place. Although this is completely possible, it is not recommended as floods, tornadoes, and other natural disasters can move a loose container.

How To: Multiple Containers

One of the biggest concerns people have when building container homes is about the size. Not everyone is cut out for living in one rectangular box. The solution to this is very simple—multiple shipping containers!

It might seem very difficult, but at its core it is relatively easy as long as they are side-by-side. Multiple containers can be used next to each other by cutting the sides out, however it is of utmost importance to reinforce and strengthen the sides that are cut out before welding the containers together.

It is also very important to have contractors do the welding of containers, as inexperienced welding can easily cause the structure to be compromised and this can lead to leaks or a home that will cave in.

Another very easy way to build with multiple containers is to use a mixture of shipping containers and traditional building techniques. With this approach, generally two or more shipping containers are put on their respective foundations. This technique then uses a brick-and-mortar structure to connect the containers, so that half of the house is a shipping container and half is a traditional building.

Shipping containers can also be stacked upon each other to create a multilevel home. The basis of attaching these together is the same attaching them side by side, and should preferably be done by a professional since they may also need to be lifted and moved by cranes or other machinery.

Step Seven: On-Site Modifications

Once the shipping containers are delivered and anchored or attached, it is time to start building. This step will encompass everything that needs to be done once the container has been fitted and fixed to the foundation.

Option One: DIY or Hiring a Contractor

If you decided to go the route of doing it yourself or hiring contractors to do it, now would be the time to start the process of adding doors and windows. Always modify the steel first, making sure to reinforce each and every cut-out so as to not compromise the structural integrity of the shipping container.

After making sure that the container is completely structurally sound, the insulation can begin. It is important to wear the necessary safety equipment and to ensure enough ventilation is in place. After inserting the insulation, wood panels or drywall are placed to give the shipping container a more finished look.

Option Two: Prefabricated

When buying a prefabricated shipping container home, the majority of the installations are already completed when the shipping container is delivered. Prefabricated shipping container homes are a much easier alternative as there is a lot less to do and a smaller chance of the insulation being incorrectly installed.

How To: Electrical

The electrical system of a shipping container home should be compliant with the National Electrical Standards (NEC) and all local laws and regulations. When electrical circuits are installed into shipping containers, it is incredibly important to have a recognized and approved electrician do it. Because a shipping container is made of pure steel, it can act as a conductor of electricity. Obviously, this means that a faulty wiring can become a major issue.

Good wiring is essential and is one of the key foundations of a shipping container home. Shipping container homes have many more challenging wiring problems than traditional houses. Electricians who have experience in building with shipping containers will best know how to install dual power, or dual and alternating currents, renewable power sources, and converters, as well as how to earth and ground any of these electrical systems.

How To: Plumbing

Making sure that a qualified person is doing the water and plumbing installations is important, because the space for these pipes is limited. Plumbing is an essential part of a shipping container home, as this installation is the key to having running water and working toilets.

In the majority of shipping container homes, the bathroom and kitchen are placed close together. Placing the two key parts of the plumbing system close together makes the installation process much easier and minimizes the number of pipes that are needed.

To have your plumbing system properly installed requires having the plumbing line within the area be established. The line will most probably be situated beneath the foundation you've laid the shipping container on. The contractor will find, determine, and mark the plumbing line before going back to the house. Next, they will prepare a passage where you want your main water line to be situated for the house and then remove any debris, dirt, and pollutants within the water line where water will be gathered from.

Ask the water contracting business for your city or county to briefly seal off the water supply so you can hook up your water line to the water supply. Cut straight to the pipeline and add your line tightly so that there are no leaks. Place your secured pipe underground and connect straight to your shipping container home. Cover up the site you had to dig up.

Once you can see the plumbing system has successfully been joined to the shipping container, hook up other portals such as the kitchen sink, restroom, lavatory, and other water channels to the correct pipes. From the central line for potable water, ensure that all pipes and taps are functioning effectively, and schedule for an analysis. Then it's time for a quick check on whether the plumbing line is working. Check the water supply to see if it has enough pressure, and test if the water is flowing well in the sink and flushing down the lavatory.

Eco-Friendly Alternatives

There are many effective alternatives when it comes to shipping container homes. Instead of using the municipal resources, you can make use of solar panels for electricity. You can also collect rainwater via downspouts from your gutters and rain barrels that can be used for bathing and flushing toilets. Collected rainwater can be purified quite easily as well and can then be used for drinking and cooking purposes.

Step Eight: Inspections

Inspections are a big part of the building process. When building has ended and there is a finished container home, building inspections need to take place. This process is essentially a final seal of approval. Many of these inspections are over quickly and you will pass fairly easily, as long as the building is up to code and hazard-free.

Step Nine: Inside and Out

The Inside:

Whether a single container or multiple, space is somewhat limited. There are more than a few tips and tricks that can help the space appear bigger and brighter.

Scale down: This tip is very easy to follow and maintain. This essentially means that when you buy furniture, it is best to buy smaller items. A great general rule of thumb is that if your furniture grazes any walls, it is too big. Try to buy minimalistic and simple items that leave a gap of air flow around the item of furniture. Furniture that has thin legs also works wonders.

Creative elements: It is always a great idea to decorate your container home in a way that makes it look much bigger on the inside. To accomplish this, place creative or artistic pieces on the walls and not the floor, as an item on the floor makes the space look more cluttered and takes away valuable floor space. Using darker creative elements that contrast against lighter walls will also make the room appear much bigger.

Mirrors: In shipping container homes, mirrors are your best friend. Strategically using mirrors can make a space look and feel bigger as the mirror reflects other elements in the home. A good rule of thumb is to place mirrors across from beds or sofas and near windows. When the mirror reflects the window, it draws the eye in, thus making the space appear much bigger.

Color theory: When it comes to painting a shipping container home, it is best to stick with a crisp white color. This color guarantees a blurring between the floor and ceiling, giving an appearance that the space is much higher than it really is. The premise of color theory is that bold furniture or art can make a small space open up considerably.

Curtains: For a shipping container home, using curtains and rugs is generally not recommended. This is because they can easily make a space feel more claustrophobic. The recommendation is to use blinds or shutters instead of curtains, and small textiles instead of large area rugs. However, if you enjoy the look of curtains and rugs in your house, it is best to stick to minimalistic items. If you still want curtains, it is possible by hanging curtains from a bar. Pull the curtains to the very sides of the window and you will still get the benefit of a seemingly bigger room, with no compromises.

Keep it simple: The key take-away here is that it is incredibly important to keep things smooth and simple in shipping container homes. Always opt for items with minimal colors and patterns so the space doesn't look crowded, cluttered, or claustrophobic. Using minimal items to draw attention to the vertical and horizontal points of the walls can also make the space appear bigger, such as linear art works or tall shelves.

Creative lighting: If it isn't possible to have windows that light up the room, getting creative with light fixtures can also work wonders. This is possible because the light draws your eyes in, making the entire room feel bigger and less claustrophobic.

The focal point: Using a single element in the middle of the room as a focal point can easily make the room feel bigger. Using a bed, table, or other piece of furniture in the center of the space will create the illusion of the room being much bigger.

The Outside

The first tip to a beautiful outside is to use wood panels on the containers. By using these as a design element, it makes the shipping container feel less industrial and homier, and also makes it easier on the eyes. Still, wood panels are not the only design element you can use, and your imagination is only limited by your budget.

One item that can beautify both the inside and outside, and even help create more internal space, are bay or bow windows. These windows project outward and provide internal shelving as well as create a stronger sense of open space and connection to the outside, much like glass doors.

Once the entire shipping container is complete, it is time to start paying attention to what surrounds the home. If the route of a rooftop garden or living roof is chosen, there are a few key elements to consider.

What is a living roof or rooftop garden? A living roof is a roof system that fosters the growth of vegetation. These vegetations can include any and all types of plants. Some types of living roofs even include complete water features and a wide array of plant species. This is also a great way to design the exterior of your home, such as planting vines to trail down your container walls from the roof, or even integrating a waterfall.

Another very good tip is to use the area around your container home to build fruit and vegetable gardens. Going this route increases the sustainability of your home and lowers the costs of food.

Some of the best tips for creating a great garden around your shipping container home are as follows:

● Seasonal: Always ensure that you are crafting your garden in a way that showcases each of the four seasons. Planting plants and flowers that bloom at different times of the year is hands-down the best tip for any do-it-yourself landscaper.

● Layers: Create three-layer patterns throughout your garden. This can be accomplished by layering three rows of flowers and plants of descending heights. Place the tallest flowers on the furthest edge, layering the smaller flowers or plants closer to the lawn.

● Evergreens: Planting evergreens around the planting beds is a very good tip; this ensures that your garden always looks full and healthy.

● Hardscapes: Just like evergreens, using hardscapes like stepping-stones, gravel, and fences will give your garden a more composed look. This will keep the garden looking full and healthy even in the winter. Fences also provide a framing effect to your house, which can make the container home look more complete.

● Water: Water features look incredible in a garden and unlike the general misconception, this garden staple is very easy to install. Water features can be bought as complete units. These complete units are easy to install and contain all of the necessary equipment. If the set does not include all components, a staff member in any garden store will be able to point you in the right direction.

Chapter 4: Budgeting

Before starting your build, it is important to understand the cost implications of a shipping container home. The first question people ask is: How much will this project cost me?

Unfortunately, there is no sort of clear-cut answer as every project will have a different price point. However, this budget template will give you a much clearer picture of what the different costs associated with your unique shipping container home will be.

Here follows a brief template of what to include in your shipping container home budget.

Why Is it Important to Know the Cost Implications?

No two projects are alike, and each person wants to know exactly what something costs before shelling out the cash. The main attraction point of shipping container homes is their affordability and cost-effectiveness. Because of this simple fact, many people can't afford to just blindly hand out cash until the project is complete.

Key Budget Parts

The Foundation

● The price of the concrete and cement that will be used to create a complete foundation.

● The formwork that will play the essential role of holding the concrete while it sets.

● The very important steel reinforcements that will ensure the foundation is strong enough to hold the heavy shipping container.

● The cost of the piles or piers will also be added here.

● The steel plates and anchors that will be used to hold the container in place.

● A complete overview of all of the labor and equipment costs that are associated with the foundation and the excavation of soil where concrete needs to be placed.

The Shell

This is the portion of the budget that covers the shipping containers themselves, plus any and all external modifications.

Superstructure

This part covers the costs of the empty shipping containers and should also include all of the delivery and offloading costs. This section of the budget should also include all of the internal and external modifications such as the following:

● The price of the insulation and creation of a good flooring base, which includes all insulation and hardwood baseboards.

● The insulation and creation of good walls and a roof. With shipping container homes, it is essential to insulate all parts of the shipping container because steel is a good conductor of temperature. Essentially, it means that a poorly insulated shipping container will be freezing in the winter and unbearably hot in the summer.

● Any structural repairs and refurbishments of heavily used containers. It is important to always be on the lookout for shipping containers that are in excellent shape, however this is not always possible. If a shipping container has significant damages, this portion will be much bigger to account for those damages.

● The reinforcement of any and all holes that have been cut into the steel of the shipping container. The amount of money included in this portion will be determined by the number of windows and doors included in your plan for the shipping container home, as well as the holes required for your plumbing and electrical systems.

● Any and all work that relates to the vertical stacking and the horizontal connection of the shipping containers. If you don't plan on using multiple shipping containers in your project, this step of the budget can be omitted.

● Any and all work that relates to bridging the gap between two parallel shipping containers. This step is only relevant if you plan on using more than one container. If your project only includes the use of one shipping container, this step becomes obsolete.

● This part of the budget will cover any and all structural support elements, like the roof decks or balconies. For this part of your budget, closely examine the chosen plan or idea; if you want to include any of these design elements, they will fall under this category of the budget.

- Any external ladders or staircases used to access other levels of the home. This can include stairs to the roof as well as stairs to the higher level of shipping containers stacked on each other. This part of the budget also hinges on whether or not you want to include balconies or second stories.

Vertical enclosure

This section of your budget will include any and all aspects that hinge on the functionality and performance elements of your shipping container home. This will only cover the non-structural modifications of the walls and shipping container. This can include all of the other items that make up the design of your shipping container home, as they don't necessarily fit into just one category. This part of the budget focuses on the design elements like the insulation on the outside that gives the shipping container home a more traditional look. This section is divided into the following subcategories:

Exterior Walls

A shipping container already has external walls, but here you will dive deeper into the non-structural elements. Any modifications to the external wall, including the outside insulation, and more traditional elements like stucco and wood used for a more traditional look, will be added here. If you add any special coatings or paint to the walls and roof, that will also be included and accounted for here.

Exterior Windows

This part of the budget is formulated especially for the windows that will be used to modify the shipping container home. Any structural support for the windows will be added to the superstructure part of the budget.

Exterior Doors

This part of the budget is formulated especially for the doors that will be used to modify the shipping container home. Any structural support will be added to the superstructure part of the budget.

Horizontal Enclosure

This is the final aspect of the shell, and this part of the budget is dedicated to all of the horizontal modifications that will take place. This part of the budget is only accounting for the design elements and not any structural elements. Any and all elements that play a role in the reinforcing or stability of the shipping container will be added into the superstructure category. This part of the budget is divided into the following categories:

Roofing

This part of your budget will include any and all aspects that are a part of the functionality of the roof. This will include any and all elements needed to make the roof more functional, like specialty paints or coatings. If you are building a secondary roof, these elements will also be included here.

Any insulation to the roof or secondary green roofs, will also be added and accounted for here. Any elements that play a role in roof-mounted solar panels as well as roof-mounted water collection tanks should be included here.

Any and all materials for a green roof would go here too, as this section focuses on all of the elements that form a part of the roofing system without necessarily being a part of the superstructure system.

Flooring

This part of your budget will focus on the non-structural elements and modifications that will form a part of the new floor. An example of this would be under-container insulation. This type of insulation works well for container floors that have been damaged, however the majority of people opt to install new flooring regardless. Installing insulated flooring helps a great deal, as it gives you more control over the temperature and can lower your electrical cost significantly.

The floors of traditional shipping containers are usually created from a mixture of woods and epoxy that is sprayed heavily with pesticides. This is dangerous for humans, however, the pesticides do dissipate over time and with that the toxic nature dissipates as well.

Interiors

The interior of a shipping container is extremely important because this is where you will spend most of your time. For the most effective budget, it is important to look at the three subcategories, which are as follows:

Interior Construction

This is the part of the budget that directly relates to turning a shipping container into an actual house; there are many aspects to this, including but not limited to:

- The framing and construction of the internal walls. This section will also include the intermediate and transitory walls, which are walls that separate the bathroom or kitchen from the rest of the house.

- The insulation of the interior of the house, with the recommended insulator being spray foam made from polyurethane.

- Any and all sub-flooring or floor insulation that will be placed or laid above the already installed flooring.

- This section will also include any doors that will be placed, like the bathroom door.

- All cupboards, countertops, and other built-in storage.

Stairs

This section will include all of the inside furnishings that will be added to the stairs of your home. This section is only relevant if it is a multi-level shipping container home and should be completely omitted in the event that a single-level shipping container home is being built.

Interior Finishes

This section of the budget will mainly focus on all of the interior design elements you can physically see and touch. There are many aspects to this, including but not limited to:

● All interior surfaces, whether on the ceiling, walls, or cupboards and countertops. This will include everything you desire to use when it comes to the interior walls and ceilings. This is important to plan thoroughly as this will prevent costs from blindsiding you during the building process. It is a very important aspect to pay close attention to as these types of costs easily escape the budgeting step.

● Paint, wallpaper, and other wall surface coatings. This will include any and all paints of other decorative aspects, and this step might require a lot of research in order to find the absolute best prices as these items can be extremely expensive.

● Flooring. The floors of many second-hand shipping containers are very damaged. This step ensures that adequate money is allocated to fixing this problem. This will be an inclusive section that focuses on any and all materials that will be used, including those to fix the flooring, or the carpets, plywood, and tiles.

● Trim, molding, and other similar architectural features. This step covers another "nice-to-have" aspect of the design process. This is a part of the process that many people choose to skip, for no other reason than finding it unnecessary.

Services

Plumbing

This section focuses on each aspect needed for functioning plumbing systems in your shipping container home. This can include a variety of different elements and will include all of the pipes, fittings, and other elements that will ensure adequate water and sewerage systems.

HVAC

This section is dedicated to all of the internal temperature systems. This will include any cooling elements like air conditioning and heating like boilers and radiators. This will also include any and all ducts that are needed to install these systems.

Fire Protection

This will include any and all systems that will relate directly towards making your building safe from fires. This can include sprinklers and smoke detectors.

Electrical

This section includes any and all systems related to the electrical implementation of the shipping container home. This section includes everything: all switches and sockets, as well as the wiring and other fixtures. It is important to pay close attention to what you will need, as the needs for an off-the-grid container and one that will be connected to the municipal systems will differ greatly.

Furnishings and Fixed Equipment

This section covers a very broad spectrum of equipment that will be needed in your home. This section can include everything from washing machines and refrigerators to vacuums and microwaves. The reason this section is so important is because people often forget to budget for this equipment, leading to costs that are not accounted for.

Sitework

This section is budgeted and accounted for at the lower portion of the budget, but it includes some of the earliest undertakings. These important activities will play a significant role in ensuring your container home is up to your standards. There are a few subcategories that form an important part of this section:

Site Preparation

This section focuses on turning a construction site from an empty plot of land to a complete building site. This will include processes like removal of vegetation and rubble, removal and demolition of existing buildings, and grading and filling of excavations to ensure a level building ground.

Site Improvements

This will include any and all modifications that have been made in order to improve the functionality and appearance of the shipping container home. These modifications can include roads and walkways, privacy and security builds, fun amenities that are not attached to the home like a pool, and all of the landscaping elements. This section provides a space for you to include all of the elements that don't have a general set category.

Mechanical Utilities

This section focuses on the systems that have to be hooked up. Many of these systems will be hooked up to the municipal main line. There are many ways to go about this section and this budget will depend on the route you decide to take. For example, you might decide to use a septic tank as opposed to a main city municipal sewerage line.

Electrical Utilities

This section will focus on everything needed to get electricity in and around your home. The list of these electrical inputs is quite long and will include the connection of all electrical wiring, as well as solar panels and wind turbines if you decide to use them. Electrical utilities also include any and all emergency generators, exterior lights, or security measures.

General

The majority of these costs will only apply if you are using a contractor or builder to complete your project. If you are doing everything yourself, some of these costs won't apply.

Taxes, Permits, Insurance, and Bonds

These costs are put into place by the local authorities or building inspectors. They will ensure that you are compliant with all of the necessary laws, rules, and regulations. These costs are important to budget for because they can cause major problems and delays if not done right and on time. These fees include, but are not limited to, the specific one-time construction fees and taxes, and all of the permit fees that relate to the necessary permits that will ensure that your project is lawful. This section will also include the necessary bonds and guarantees from a building contractor.

Fees and Contingencies

These fees relate directly to the final fees that are needed for a shipping container home. These fees will include all of the design fees like the architect, all of the engineering fees, and contingencies. A contingency budget is extremely important; having a 20% contingency budget will allow for any unforeseen or cost emergencies to be accounted for. This section of the budget does not have to be complete or thought out, but this amount is often essential in the building process.

The Next Steps

After the process of setting up and completing a budget estimate, there are few other things to do. The following steps will help to ensure that your budget is up to standard and that there are no surprises when the building commences. Even if building a shipping container home is more affordable, it is still a big cost. For the best results, it is important to do research thoroughly and to shop around. This will guarantee that you pay the best prices for all of the elements that go into building and designing a shipping container home.

Verify Your Estimate

Every evaluation or quote requires an immediate check. This makes sure the assessment isn't fully off base and worthless.

Whether through data entry failure or just poor guesses, it's easy to unintentionally end up with an assessment that is way off of reasonable rates.

To conduct an estimate check, correlate your evaluation to something else. Examples include:

● Analyzing the predicted costs with those generated by other estimate types, which can be achieved using online sites.

- Comparing your assessment to those generated by friends or relatives. This can work to establish that you are forming a bias-free evaluation.

- Comparing your assessment to the costs of alternative container homes you've seen.

- Running your estimation by someone trained in construction.

Save Information about Your Estimate

If your assessment passes the check, you know it's at least worth considering as a starting point. So, the next step is saving your estimate.

An estimate is only as good as the values you use, so you have to record the inputs you used to make it. Additionally, any information you have on why you chose those inputs and values is helpful and will benefit you in the future.

As the days and weeks go by, details will slowly slip from your memory. But it's likely you'll want to go back and revisit an estimate as you move through your project, modify the design, or when additional money becomes available for the project.

Here are a few examples of information we recommend you record with your estimate:

● When did you create the estimate?

● What is the project?

● Why did you include these specific values?

Update Your Estimate with New Ideas and Information

Updating your budget continually is important because things will often change. This way of going about your budget can ensure that you're always ready for any new challenges you may face during building.

The two main types of price changes you may face are internal and external changes. Internal changes are the changes you have control over; these are the choices you make that influence your budget. External changes are those you have no control over; these are changes that happen outside of your decisions and will still impact your budget.

The Take-Away

The general take-away here is that it is important to budget around all of the items that could possibly be used in your shipping container home, even if you think it might not be necessary. So many costs are usually overlooked and are surprising when they appear once building commences because the first budget was not done thoroughly.

Some items of this budget can be omitted to suit the particular style, structure, or route you decide to take. These can include when people decide to use prefabricated shipping container homes and when people decide on certain other things like how many shipping containers they want, how many levels, and even the amount of design and creative elements their shipping container home will include.

The process of building a shipping container home is not easy and should never be taken lightly because even the smallest mistakes can cost a fortune to fix.

Chapter 5: Frequently Asked Questions

What Is the Strength of the Concrete Needed for a Foundation?

This will generally be determined by the geo-technical engineer or contractor that is on site. Concrete strength is referred to as the C value. These values each have their own formulas, the most common ones are as follow:

- C15: This is a general all-purpose concrete and is made by mixing one part cement, two parts sand, and five parts gravel.

- C30: This is an incredibly strong concrete, and it is composed of one part cement, two parts sand, and three parts gravel.

If you are mixing the concrete in small quantities, then it can be made either by hand or using a cement mixer. The concrete needs to be completely and thoroughly mixed in order to retain structural integrity.

How Much Concrete Do I Need?

Figuring out how much concrete you need is a pretty straightforward calculation. By using the measurements of the area where the concrete goes, you can get a very accurate cubic meter reading. The formula is as follows: multiply the width by the height by the depth (width x height x depth).

How Does the Curing Process Work?

The curing process works by drying out the moisture in the concrete. This moisture comes from the water that is added to the cement mix. Concrete only cures if it is in a certain temperature range, and this information can be found on the packaging. If the temperature is lower than the recommendation, the use of cling wrap can be employed to give more heat. It typically takes between five and seven days for concrete to fully cure and during this time the concrete needs to be kept moist.

How to Pour Concrete in Hot Weather?

If the climate is very hot, it is very important to prepare the site before pouring the concrete. This can be accomplished by placing sunshades to block any direct contact with the sun. It is also important to mix the concrete with cold water and to spray the area where the concrete will go with cold water. The best time to pour concrete in humid climates is in the early mornings or late afternoons; avoid pouring concrete in peak temperatures.

How to Pour Concrete in Cold Weather?

Just like pouring concrete in hot weather, there are a few precautions to take before pouring concrete in cold climates. Cold weather in this context is categorized as the average temperature being below zero for three consecutive days. Before pouring any concrete, make sure that all ice and snow have been cleared from the area. It is also very important to remove any standing water. Once the concrete has been poured, lay down insulating blankets right away. Use the blankets or cling wrap for three to seven days until the concrete is completely cured. Once the concrete is cured, remove the blankets gradually over the course of a few days. If you remove the blankets too fast, the temperature change will cause the concrete to crack.

Are Green Roofs Safe?

There is a widely accepted misconception that green or living roofs will cause structures to be compromised and that they will cause the roof of your shipping container to leak. This is completely false. If installed correctly, green roofs are completely safe and damage free. There is a lot of evidence that points to these types of roofs being a lot safer and that they can actually delay the deterioration processes of your home. Because these roofs give you an added layer of protection from the sun, and with the water-proofing membrane, they work incredibly well at keeping ultraviolet rays from reaching the steel of the container roof.

How Long Will My Shipping Container Home Last?

There are a variety of factors. The general lifespan of a converted shipping container is around a hundred years. Traditional houses can reach this age as well, and there is no guarantee that a shipping container home will last longer than its counterparts. Something that can play a very big role in how long your shipping container home will last is corrosion.

Corrosion is a deep form of damage to the steel, and this term refers to so much more than just rust. When steel corrodes, it slowly dissolves thanks to the sea, water, and other pollutants that they come into contact with. Once corrosion starts, there are no quick fixes, and it can cost thousands to repair. The only metals that can't corrode are silver, gold, and platinum.

Corten steel is a good alternative. This type of steel is highly corrosion-resistant and widely used in the creation of shipping containers. This steel can withstand extreme weather. When Corten steel starts to oxidize it can look like it is beginning to rust, however this oxidation process stops, and the steel is never damaged. Shipping containers are generally created from

Corten steel because it is 40% stronger than normal steel and in some cases that number can skyrocket up to 75%.

Is There a Resale Market for Shipping Container Homes?

The resale market is big for shipping container homes, with demand growing steadily. This makes a shipping container home an incredibly good investment opportunity.

Is it Safe?

The short answer here is yes, it is completely safe to convert and live inside of a shipping container. The key here is to make sure that the shipping container meets all of the necessary building codes and that it passes all of the inspections with flying colors. Inspections and building codes are a pain to just about every person that has to deal with them, but at the end of it all, the only reason for these rules is to protect the occupants of the home. Some shipping containers carry toxic chemicals, and for that reason it is incredibly important to research and find out as much as you can about the shipping container and the suppliers of those shipping containers.

Are all Shipping Containers Created Equal?

The easy answer here is yes, all shipping containers are created according to worldwide ISO standards. This governing body ensures that each and every shipping container can stand up to the rigorous tests that they will face while on the ocean. Although these shipping containers are all created equally, they can still have many issues due to the environment and their journeys. Shipping containers face a lot of problems on the ocean, and because of this it is best to buy shipping containers that have only had one trip on the ocean. Shipping containers that have had multiple trips are more prone to the harmful effects that salt water has on steel, namely corrosion. Corrosion is an expensive problem to fix.

What Is the Biggest Potential Downfall?

The biggest potential downfall are the hidden costs. These can easily be incurred if the budget of the contractor isn't thoroughly explained to the consumer. A very good example of this is how many transport companies don't explain each of their fees and services. This can lead to a miscommunication between client and consumer that easily lets the consumer pay much more than expected for a simple service. This happens very often in the construction industry and many first-time clients are not aware of these potential downfalls.

Why Do I Need an Insulator?

The reason why it is so incredibly important to use a good insulator is because of the way heat and cold can impact steel. When faced with too much heat or cold, the temperature in the shipping container will drastically change. This can cause a significant rise in the electricity usage of the homeowner. For this reason, it is beneficial to insulate a shipping container so it will regulate heat and cold efficiently.

How Do I Make My Shipping Container Home Eco-Friendly?

For many people, this is one of their biggest goals: having a shipping container home that is completely and utterly eco-friendly. This can easily be done by making a few small changes like:

- Solar panels: These panels that are installed on the roof of a home work by capturing the sunlight and converting it into electricity to be used in the home. This is a great investment as it will eventually pay for itself in the way of very-low-to-no municipal cost for the use of electricity. The benefits also include very low maintenance costs.

● Rainwater storage: Rainwater can be collected and stored.

This essentially free water can then be used for toilets, bathing, and to water vegetation. There are many ways to filter this water and it can then be used as drinking water too. This form of water supply is very beneficial as it can reduce or even eliminate the need for municipal water.

● Vegetable garden: Many people who buy and create shipping

container homes intend to live off the grid. Because of this, there are many plans available to create vegetable gardens around your shipping container home, and the most popular is by using a vegetable garden as a living roof.

Is it Very Hard to Build a Shipping Container Home?

The popular misconception is that building a shipping container is extremely difficult. The truth, however, is that it is just as hard to build a traditional house as it is to build a shipping container home. The one thing that separates a failed shipping container conversion from a good one is research. The reason for this is because of how easily people get misled into believing and thinking in a certain way. If you do enough research on the topic, then building your dream shipping container home is very easy. A popular saying is that "nothing worth having comes easy," and that is absolutely the key here.

When you put in the hours and time to learn about the industry and trade, the entire process will seem much simpler.

What Is Value Engineering and How Can it Benefit Me?

Value engineering, or cost engineering as it is often referred to, is a form of building construction that has a complete balance between the cost, speed, and quality. This style of construction is incredibly effective because it ensures that you get the best possible product for the least amount of money and time.

Value engineering puts a very big focus on the amount of function and functionality to be found in a building project and also aims to reduce costs once the house has been completely built. For this to work, it is important to take a look at the custom versus standardized elements in your design.

When it comes to windows, it is more cost-effective to use standardized frames and windows as opposed to using custom-built ones, but when it comes to flooring, the opposite is usually true. For flooring it is often beneficial to install more expensive flooring as it lasts longer and will save money in the long run.

Conclusion

Thanks for taking the time to read this book on shipping container homes.

You should now have a good understanding of the many benefits of building a shipping container home, as well as what's required to do so.

Hopefully the process now seems a lot simpler, and you're feeling motivated to start designing your very own container home!

www.ingramcontent.com/pod-product-compliance
Lightning Source LLC
LaVergne TN
LVHW011738060526
838200LV00051B/3239